Introduction

Whether you've never tried pyrography before or you've simply used it for small projects and want to refresh yourself on the techniques, this booklet will show you how to create beautiful pieces with only a pyrographic tool. Today's pyrographic equipment can be both inexpensive and readily available, so getting started is easy to do.

Although it is often referred to as woodburning, the art of pyrography can be worked on just about any natural surface, which gives you a wide variety of possibilities on which to explore this craft. Wooden box tops, gourd bluebird houses, watercolor paper that's suitable for framing, and even leather belts are used as working surfaces for burned designs. For this booklet, I worked the finished samples on several different species of wood, such as birch plywood and basswood. However, the techniques and instructions do apply to other materials, such as leather, paper, and gourds.

As you work your way through the booklet, we will explore what materials and tools you will need for your woodburning kit and how to practice creating and controlling woodburned tonal values through the use of textures and layers. The booklet ends with a section of exercises and accompanying projects, giving you the opportunity to apply what you have learned. With the basic instructions in this book and a little practice, you will soon be able to woodburn any project with confidence and expertise.

Table of Contents

ISBN 978-1-57421-505-2

Pyrography Basics contains content first published by Fox Chapel Publishing in 2006 in the book *Great Book of Woodburning* and in 2012 in the book *The Art & Craft of Pyrography*.

© 2014 by Lora S. Irish and New Design Originals, www.d-originals.com, an imprint of Fox Chapel Publishing, 800-457-9112, 1970 Broad Street, East Petersburg, PA 17520.

Printed in China
First printing

What is Pyrography?

Pyrography: The art of burning a design or pattern into a natural surface, such as wood, gourds, leather, or cotton rag watercolor paper using heated one-temperature or variable-temperature woodburning tools or a fine flame.

Pyrography Systems

There are two types of pyrography systems—the one-temperature unit and the variable-temperature system.

One-temperature tools heat to a pre-set temperature and create tonal value by controlling your texture or burn strokes and by the speed of your burning stroke.

Variable-temperature tools allow you to adjust the temperature of the tips from a very cool setting to extremely hot.

The number of distinct tonal values that can easily be created increases with the variable temperature tool because you control how cool or hot the tip is during the work.

One-temperature tools

Once plugged into an electrical outlet, the tool quickly reaches an even but high temperature, so the textures you make, the strokes that you use, and the speed of the stroke control the tonal value work in your project.

Using a light pressure to the tip against the wood and moving the tool tip quickly through the burn stroke creates very pale tonal values. Medium pressure and slower motion bring darker tones. One-temperature burning tools are inexpensive, readily available at your local craft or hobby store, and excellent for first-time pyrographers to give the craft a try.

Options. From single- to variable-temperature units, pyrographers can choose from many options. Your skill level, your goals as an artist or craftsman, and your budget are among the factors that will influence your decision.

Pen types. Pens with tips allow you to increase your inventory of tip shapes without spending a lot of money. Fixed-tip pens (blue grip above) eliminate any heat or energy loss where the tip connects with the unit.

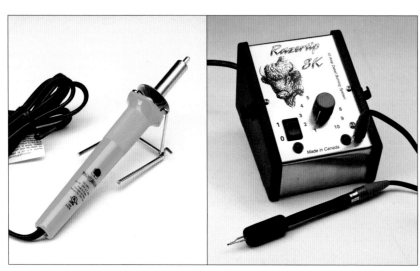

Temperature control. The single-temperature burner on the left takes time to heat up, but holds its temperature well. The variable-temperature burner on the right heats up—and cools—quickly.

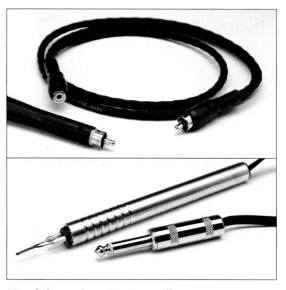

Handpiece wires. Most woodburners use an RCA plug (top photo) to connect the burning pen to the handpiece wire. Some units (bottom photo) use a ¼" (0.5cm)-diameter phone jack for the connection.

Variable-temperature burners

Variable-temperature systems have a dial thermostat that allows you to control how cool or hot your tip is. You can adjust the temperature setting quickly, making it easy to control your tonal values in your project. This style has two types of pens—the fixed-tip pen, where the tip is permanently set in the handgrip, and the interchangeable pen, where different wire tips can be used with the handgrip. There are many excellent burning systems available to the hobbyist. Which manufacturer you chose depends on your budget, your pen style preferences, and what is available to you locally or online.

Dual-pen system. With a dual-pen system, plug two pens, each with a different tip, into the unit during any burning session. A selector switch allows the user to change from one pen to the other and a thermostat controls the temperature setting for whichever tip is in use.

The pens for this unit are slim and lightweight, making it comfortable for long sessions of burning. The lead wire that goes from the pen to the burning unit is permanently affixed to the pen's end. The handgrip area may be covered with foam wrap or cork to reduce the heat that reaches the hand.

Single-pen unit. Many single-pen units have a range of temperature settings. Changing fixed pens or changing tips on the interchangeable pens is quick and easy. The temperature dial system is very reliable for quick tonal value changes. This particular unit can reach very hot temperatures and working to the extreme black tones is simply a matter of turning up the heat.

The cork handles are very comfortable and dramatically reduce the heat transfer from the tip to your hand. This style uses a positive, tight connector at the front of the pen for the interchangeable-tip pen making the exchange of tips easy.

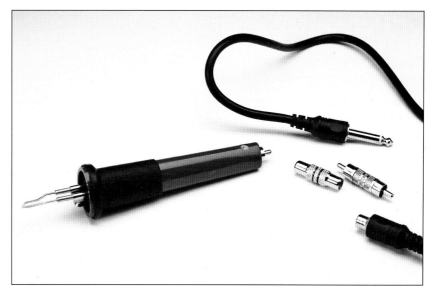

Adaptability. Most manufacturers sell adapters that allow you to use other manufacturers' pens with their control units. Some units come with a full set of adapters.

Pen grips. The thick blue foam on the pen above insulates the user's fingers from the heat of the pen. Vents and distance on the pen below move the user's fingers back from the hottest part of the pen.

For detailed reviews and more information about pyrography machines, visit the "Pyrography Machine Buyer's Guide" at www.pyrographyonline.com.

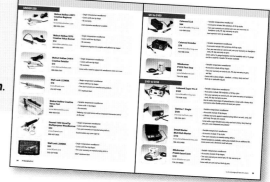

Pyrography Tips

Tips comes in many shapes and bends, from the tight bend used in the standard writing tip to half circles that can create fish scales and even square tubes that make a textured pattern on your board. Three basic pen tips are used throughout this book—the standard writing tip, the micro writing tip, and a small flat spoon shader.

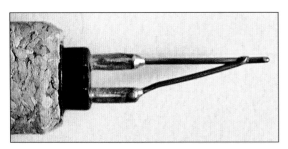

Standard writing tip pen. For wide line shading and texture work, try the standard writing tip. By holding the pen in an upright position, 90° from the working surface, fine detail lines can be pulled. To create wider lines in your texturing, drop your grip to about 45° from the wood. The angle change allows the side of the wire to touch the board giving you more metal to wood contact.

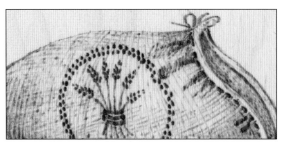

Standard tip sample. The standard tip pen creates a strong, wide line perfect for both outlining and shading.

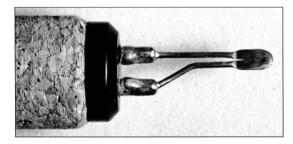

Micro writing tip pen. The micro writing tool is manufactured using thinner wire and a tighter bend at the tip than the standard writing tool. The tip's shape allows little metal to come into direct contact with the working surface and produces fine detailing lines. Fine dense textures can be layered using this tool to burn an area into an even, smooth tonal value.

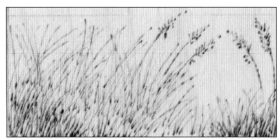

Micro tip sample. For extremely fine line work, try the micro tip pen.

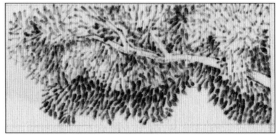

Spoon shader tip pen. This small flat shader creates a wide path of smooth tonal values and is excellent for general shading within your design. Shader tips come in several profiles, from spoon shaped, square, and half rounds.

Spoon shader sample. Large areas can quickly be toned using the spoon shaped shading tip.

General Supplies

You will want to gather a small tool kit of craft supplies for your pyrography. Many of these items are common household items you may already have on hand.

For sanding:

- Sandpaper, from 220- to 320-grit
- Sanding pads
- Foam core fingernail files

Your wood surfaces need a light sanding to create a smooth surface for burning. Use fine-grit sandpaper, 220- to 320-grit, to remove the fine ridges and loose fibers on the wood. Coarse sandpaper, less than 220-grit, can leave sanding lines that can affect the quality of your burn lines. Even fine ridges will cause your tool tip to skip or move as you pull the stroke, resulting in uneven or non-straight lines.

Sanding pads have a foam core and are flexible, making them great for curved surfaces as on a wood plate or the routed edge of a plaque. Available at your local drug store, foam core fingernail files are a nice addition to your tool kit.

For cleaning tool tips

- Emery cloth or silicon carbide cloth
- Fine steel wool
- Leather strop, strop rouge, red oxide or aluminum oxide

It is important to keep your tool tips well cleaned during any burning session to ensure even heat to the tip and consistent color tones to your burning. As you work, notice the tool tips become dark or dull as carbon from the burning builds up on the wire. The carbon can affect the heat coming from the tip to the wood and leave black carbon smudges on your work. Clean the tips of your tools often.

Scraping the tip with a special tool provided by the manufacturer or with a sharpened knife can quickly clean the tip. Emery cloth, fine steel wool, or a woodcarving leather strop prepared with either red oxide rouge or with aluminum oxide are alternatives.

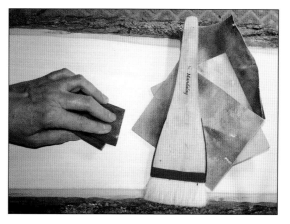

Smooth surface. Sanding wood surfaces before tracing your pattern onto the medium ensures as smooth a working surface as possible. Paper, cloth, and leather do not require sanding.

Cleaning your tips. There are several methods for cleaning the wire tips of the variable temperature tool.

For tracing:

- Pencils
- Colored ink pen
- Carbon or graphite paper
- Transparent tape

Two products used to transfer the design to your work surface are carbon and graphite papers.

Both products are laid under your paper pattern so that the transfer side is against your work surface. Both should be used carefully, as they are not easily removed from your work surface after burning is complete. Graphite paper, with its soft pale grey coloring, is especially appropriate for gourds, papier-mâché, and darker woods.

You can also blacken the back of your pattern paper with a soft pencil, covering it completely. Place the pattern onto your work surface and trace over the pattern lines, leaving a fine line of pencil graphite on your work surface. The pencil lines can later be removed with a white artist eraser.

And generally...

- White artist eraser
- Transparent tape
- Dusting brush
- Old toothbrush
- Assorted soft paintbrushes
- Ceramic tile or wood palette
- Rulers and straight edge
- T-square or right angle triangle
- Cardboard
- Canvas stretchers
- Long quilter's straight pins
- Bench knife or utility knife
- X-Acto knife
- Small round gouge

Many common household items and tools are used for pyrography to prepare the working surface, secure your pattern, trace the design, and finish the completed burning.

If you will be adding paint to your finished burning, you will need an assortment of soft bristle brushes, a paint palette, water pans, and, of course, the thinning media for whichever type of paint you have chosen to use.

Bench knives or X-Acto knives can be used to carefully carve away small mistakes in the burning and to cut fine highlight lines into an area that has already been burned. Some pyrographers also use them as scrapers to clean the tool tips.

When working on cotton canvas, you will want several sheets of heavy cardboard and long quilter's straight pins to secure the cloth so that you are working on a tight, non-moving surface. Canvas stretchers can be purchased at your local art store so that you can secure large pieces of canvas fabric.

Also include in your kit white artist erasers. Please avoid pink erasers, as they can leave pink streaks of color on your work surface that are not easily removed. The white eraser cleans up any leftover tracing lines and any oil or dirt from your hands that builds up during a burning session.

Large dusting brushes are excellent for removing the dust created during the preparation stage of sanding your wood surface. Old toothbrushes can also be used; they are also useful in removing any excess rouge from your tool tips during preparation.

BASIC SUPPLY LIST:

- Single-temperature solid-tip tool
- Variable-temperature units
- Standard writing tip pen
- Micro writing tip pen
- Medium or spoon shader tip pen
- Sandpaper
- Sanding pads, 220- to 320-grit
- Foam core fingernail files
- Emery cloth or silicon carbide cloth
- Fine steel wool
- Leather strop, strop rouge
- Pencils

- Colored ink pen
- Carbon or graphite paper
- Transparent tape
- White artist eraser
- Dusting brush
- Old toothbrush
- Assorted soft paintbrushes
- Ceramic tile
- Rulers and straight edge
- T-square or right angle triangle
- Cardboard or chipboard
- Canvas stretchers
- Long quilter's straight pins
- Bench knife or utility knife

- X-Acto knife
- Small round gouge
- Acrylic spray sealer
- White glue
- Hot glue gun
- Fabric paint
- Artist colored pencils
- Watercolor pencils

Creating a Wood Practice Board

One of the fun ways to learn to control your woodburning strokes is to create a practice board. This gives you a working surface on which to experiment with the wide variety of strokes you will use. It can also be used to record any new strokes and layering techniques you discover as you grow in this craft. Plus, because this board is only used as practice, it is a great place to work until you learn to control your strokes. Once you have control over the stroke, you can move to your working project with confidence.

I also use my practice board to work out textures and specific elements of a pattern. Small pattern samples not only let me create the textures I want to use, but also help me establish the lights and darks in a pattern before I start on my actual project.

My practice boards are usually made on birch plywood because this is the wood species that I use the most. You may wish to make your practice board on your favorite wood surface so your practice work will show you the same burns as those on your finished projects.

The most basic practice board, and the one I recommend all beginning pyrographers create, is laid out as a grid pattern on the wood. I used a soft #2 pencil and a T-square to section my board into 1" (2.5cm) squares with ¼" (0.5cm) spacing between each square. As you begin each new project or approach a texture that you have not done before, try it out first on your practice board. Number each square with a pencil so you may keep a corresponding card file for each square, noting the particular tool tip you used, the temperature settings for the burner, and on which project you used the texture.

Keep your practice board close to your work area. This makes it quick and easy to add new textures, and it will be handy for choosing previously tested textures for a new project.

Creating textures. Mark a 10" x 12" (25.5 x 30.5cm) sheet of poplar or birch plywood or a piece of basswood into five rows of 1" (25mm) squares with a pencil. Use the grid squares to create each new texture.

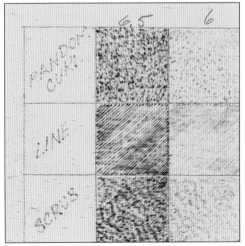

Marking the board. Make pencil notations on your practice board for both the temperature setting and pen tip used.

Temperature settings

In the example (left), for my first row (right row A) I set the burner temp setting at 5 and then filled the top square with a random curling doodle stroke. The square below it was worked on setting 6, then setting 7 through to setting 9. With each temperature change, the tonal value becomes darker. I have marked my temperature setting in pencil to the right of each square for easy reference later.

Three Common Fill Patterns

Three common fill patterns used in pyrography are crosshatching, random doodles, and the scrubbie stroke.

Crosshatching fills an area with layers of fine parallel lines. Each new layer is laid on a diagonal to the last, slowly developing the depth of the tonal value.

Make the **random doodle stroke** by working tightly packed loops. As the new looping line crosses an older line, the area becomes denser and therefore darker.

The **scrubbie** is a short back-and-forth stroke that quickly fills an area. The space between each of those back-and-forth strokes, how much unburned area is allowed, establishes your tonal depth.

As you work your practice board, you will discover the fill strokes that are the most comfortable or natural for you to use in your style of work.

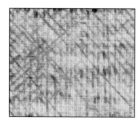

Crosshatch Texture

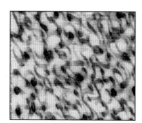

Random Doodle

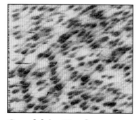

Scrubbie Stroke

By creating a practice board that you keep close to your work area, you can test new textures, tonal values, and even small pieces of a design before you begin work on your project surface. Try creating the practice board pictured on page 9 by following this chart.

Quick Reference Texture Chart

Square #	Texture Name	Tonal Value
1–5	Dash Stroke	Pale to dark tones
6–14	Linear Circles	Pale value to dark tones
15–23	Wide-Spaced Crosshatch	Medium to black tones
24–32	Tight-Spaced Crosshatch	Medium to black tones
33–37	Random Curls	Pale to dark tones
38	Check Marks	Medium to dark tones
39	Wide-Spaced Zigzag	Medium tone
40	Random Zigzag	Medium tone
41	Sun Rays or Grass Strokes	Medium tone
42	Wavy Lines	Medium to dark tones
43	Seashell Circles	Dark tones
44	Tightly Packed Zigzag	Medium tone
45	Tight Circles	Medium to dark tones
46	ABC	Dark tone
47	568	Dark tone
48	Scales	Dark tone
49	SUE	Medium to dark tones
50	Mountain Peaks	Dark tone
51	Quilting	Medium tone
52	Overlapping Hearts	Medium tone
53	Herringbone	Medium to dark tones
54	Diagonal Ripples	Medium to dark tones
55	Water Ripples	Medium to dark tones
56	Tightly Packed Spots	Dark to black tones
57	Long Scales	Dark to black tones
58	Close-up Branches and Leaves	Medium to black tones
59	Wood Grain	Pale to dark tones
60	Tall Grass Clumps	Medium to dark tones
61–64	Scrubby Lines	Pale to dark tones
65	Small Crosshatched Elements	Pale to dark tones
66–68	Straight Lines	Pale to dark tones
69	Long Curved Line	Pale to dark tones
70	Short Curved Line	Pale to dark tones
71	Veining Curved Line	Pale to dark tones
72	Background Trees	Medium to dark tones
73	Tall Grass	Pale to dark tones
74	Stone Walkway	Medium tones
75	Evergreens	Pale to dark tones
76	Deciduous Trees	Pale to dark tones
77	Pines and Deciduous Shrubs	Pale to dark tones
78	Roof and Shadows	Pale to dark tones
79	Barn Boards	Pale to dark tones
80	Bricks	Pale to dark tones
81	Small Pine and Shrub	Pale to dark tones

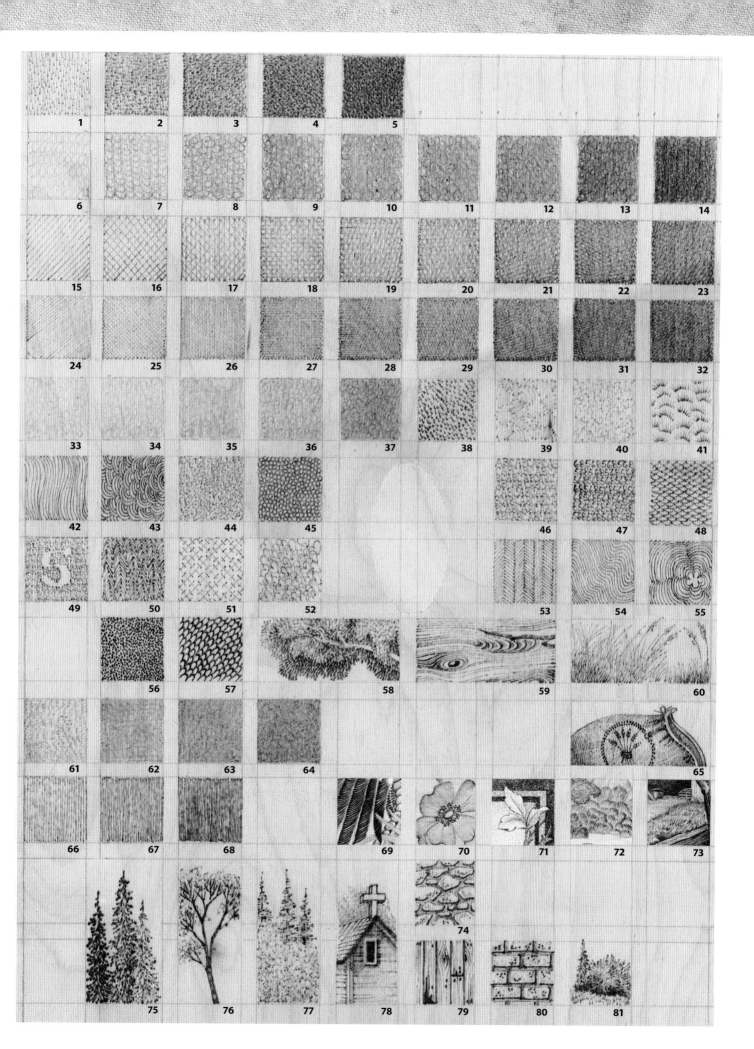

Tonal Values Practice Board

(Uses pattern on page 13.)

Tonal or gray scale values refer to how dark or light a burned area appears in your work. The palest values in a woodburning are those not burned at all. Instead, the raw wood is used for the sepia tone of that area. The darkest tonal value will be areas you burn at high temperatures to a near black tone. A range of tones, from pale tans to mid-browns and on into dark browns, falls between the two extremes.

This range of tonal values, worked from the palest progressively through the mid-tones into the black, is called a tonal value scale. Tonal value scales are called gray scales when you are working with black-and-white photographs. For woodburnings, they are called sepia value scales because of the soft beige through rich deep browns of the burned wood.

In woodburning, how pale or dark your tonal value for an area becomes depends on the temperature setting of your burning unit, the time the tip touches the wood, and how loosely or tightly packed your burn strokes are in an area.

The tiger portrait is divided into five tonal values:

- **black** for around the eyes, nose, and mouth
- **dark** for the wide facial stripes
- **medium** for the shading along the sides of his face, chin, and nose
- **pale** for light shading through the nose, forehead, and under the eyes
- **white** (unburned) areas in what would be the white stripes of his face.

Bengal Tiger. A study in tonal value scales on wood.

SUPPLIES:

- 8" x 8" (20 x 20cm) birch plywood
- variable-temperature burning unit
- standard writing tip
- matte acrylic spray sealer

Sepia Value Scale for Bengal Tiger

1 Dark tonal value. After tracing the pattern to the wood, I worked my dark tonal values using a medium-high temperature setting. For my unit, that is a setting between 6 and 6.5 on my dial. I used a tightly packed short line stroke that was worked with the direction of the wood grain. As I worked, I moved the tool tip in a slow, smooth motion across the wood. The slow motion, tightly packed strokes, and medium-high setting gave me an even deep brown tonal value.

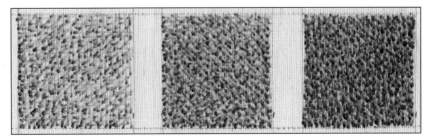

Scrubbie stroke. The scrubbie stroke is made with a quick back and forth motion. The number of small scrubbie lines, the temperature setting, and the number of layers of burning determine the tonal value.

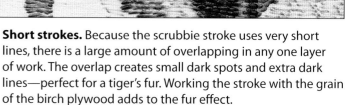

Short strokes. Because the scrubbie stroke uses very short lines, there is a large amount of overlapping in any one layer of work. The overlap creates small dark spots and extra dark lines—perfect for a tiger's fur. Working the stroke with the grain of the birch plywood adds to the fur effect.

2 **Medium tonal value.** To lighten the tonal value in the next areas to be burned, I turned down my temperature setting to just below 6, a medium setting for my unit. Otherwise, I used the same slow movement with the grain to burn the tightly packed short line strokes. The simple adjustment to my temperature setting created a new tonal value of medium brown.

3 **Pale tonal value.** For my pale value burned areas, I turned down my temperature setting to about 5.5, a low-medium setting for my unit. I increased the speed of my burning motion. This kept the tool tip on the wood for a minimal amount of time. I also allowed more space between each short line stroke. This small amount of space allows some of the raw wood to show through the burned area, helping to keep this area in a pale tan tonal value.

4 **Black tonal value.** My black tones were worked last by turning my temperature back to 6.5 and by using a very slow motion with the tool tip. Again, I used a tightly packed short line stroke to fill the areas around the eyes, nostrils, and mouth. I now have a completed burning with little or no texture and no outlining or detailing. The entire pattern was worked by using only four burned tonal values and the white of the raw, unburned wood. With tonal values alone I created a Bengal tiger's face. The completed project has distinct tonal values from the white of the wood through the black tones surrounding the eyes.

© Lora S. Irish

Bengal Tiger
Pattern shown at actual size.

Exercises for Practice

Now that you know how to create different tonal values and textures and have worked on a practice board, I wanted to give you some exercises to practice some of the different techniques. Go ahead and try the whole pattern if you want, or you can just try parts of the pattern to further explore its listed skill. Unless otherwise stated, the practice projects in this section were worked using a variable-temperature tool with the writing tip on birch plywood. If you are working with a one-temperature tool, please use the universal tip. Heat settings are noted for each project.

Light and Dark Exercise One: Temperature of the Tip

The wheat design used in *Our Daily Bread* (pattern on page 16) is created with a simple straight-line fill texture (see the photos at the right and Squares 66–68 on page 9). The coloring of each line in the wheat—whether it is light, medium, or dark—is controlled by the temperature of the tool. Notice in this finished sample that all of the woodburned lines run vertically within the design and that no element of the pattern has been outlined.

Tips for completing the entire pattern:

- Use a medium-high or high setting to burn the sections that are turned back on the bottom cross leaves and the tall pale leaves.
- The lettering is done in very close, tightly packed, short lines to create the darkest burning on the board.

Our Daily Bread. Even though this burning uses only one texture, the straight line, it has three distinct tonal values: dark, medium, and light. How cool or hot you set your variable-temperature tool determines the tonal value of the burned stroke.

1 **Here is a small wheat pattern** that you can use on your practice board to learn to control the tonal values through your temperature settings on your variable-temperature tool.

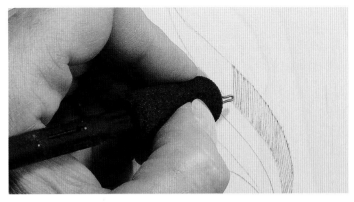

2 **Once the sample pattern has been traced**, set your thermostat to a very low setting. Start your project with the tallest pale leaf. Pull long, light-colored lines from the top of the leaf to the bottom section, touching the traced line at both points. Fill that leaf with closely packed parallel lines using your writing tip.

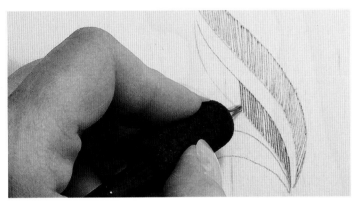

3 **Turn your thermostat up** to a medium temperature setting. Fill the second wheat leaf with parallel lines using the writing tip. Notice that these lines burn slightly darker than the lines in the first leaf.

4 **By turning up your thermostat one more time** to a medium-high or high setting, you can now fill the last, third leaf with dark-toned lines.

5 **The wheat head** has three rows of seeds. The center row is burned using a low setting; the right-side row uses a medium setting; and the left-side row, the stem, and the wheat whiskers are burned at a medium-high or high setting.

6 **Once all of the burning is done**, use a white artist's eraser to remove any remaining pencil graphite from the tracing and very lightly sand the surface with an emery board. Because each area was created using the same texture—the straight-line fill—the pattern's depth of color was established solely through the temperature settings of the tool.

Our Daily Bread
Pattern shown at actual size.

© Lora S. Irish

Light and Dark Exercise Two: Burning Time

For the pattern *Wild Rose Corner*, on page 22, the thermostat for the woodburning tool was set at a medium range throughout the work (see the photos at the right). The changes in the coloring—the darkness of the wide borderline to the lightness of the leaves—were determined by how long the tool remained on the wood during the burning. Slow strokes created the dark areas; faster strokes made light lines.

Wild Rose Corner. A wide range of values can be created just by learning to control how much time you use to make an individual burned stroke.

Tips for completing the entire pattern:

- Begin by working the texture pattern that lies behind the borderlines and flower design. This texture is a simple swirl design, created by moving your tool in very small, random curls across the wood (see Squares 33–37 on page 9). Start this curl pattern at the inner corner of the wide borderline; this is your darkest area for the background work. Move the tool slowly throughout this area to burn a medium-toned coloring. As you work away from the corner toward the outside of the pattern area, increase the speed with which you move your tool. Slightly faster burning will create paler curled lines. Continue filling in the background, gradually increasing the speed of your stroke until you can barely see the burn lines along the farthest edges of the work.

- The stems on the rose are done with short straight-line fill strokes (see Squares 66–68 on page 9), allowing the tool to touch the wood long enough to create a medium-dark tone. The dark shading in the rose stems is done by repeating the burning over these areas. This gives two layers to the shaded side of the stem.

- The outline on the flower petals is darker at the base of the flower and becomes pale toward the outer edge.

- The veins in the flower petals, rosebud, flower center, and leaves are done in gently curved lines (see Squares 69–70 on page 9) at a medium stroke speed.

- Work the petal lines from both the outer edge of the petal toward the center and then from the center of the petal toward the flower center, creating two sets of lines within each petal.

- Work the flower center from the central circle.

- Use tightly packed spots (see Square 56 on page 9) to create small dots on the center lines of the rose and in the deep areas of the rosebud.

1 **This three rose leaf pattern** will let you learn how the speed of the tool affects the tonal value of the burned line or area. As with the exercise for *Our Daily Bread*, this small design can be worked on your practice board.

2 **Trace the design** to your practice board. Set the temperature of your variable-temperature tool to a medium heat. Start by outlining the leaves. Move the tool slowly so that the tool tip can burn a dark line along the edge of each leaf. Increase your speed as you approach a stop area. Notice where the leaf notches touch. The line closest to that joint is darker than the line at the tip of the leaf.

3 **Begin the stroke at the center vein** and pull your tool toward the outer edge of the leaf. The veins are done in gently curved lines (see Squares 69–70 on page 9) at a medium stroke speed. Notice how the line is darkest where it touches the center vein and then pales as you pull the tool away from that vein. This happens because your tool tip is hottest when it first touches the wood. As the tip is pulled through a stroke it begins to cool slightly, therefore lightening the end of the burned line. You can use this to your advantage in a design. Starting the stroke, its darkest point, at the center vein area of a leaf, for example, gives emphasis to the center vein.

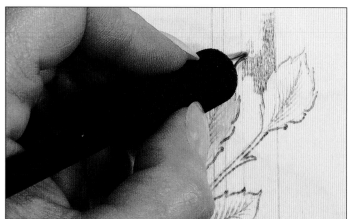

4 **The large wide line** behind the leaves is worked with a scrubby line texture and even, smooth movement.

5 **Watch the color of the burning** as you begin working this area. If the color seems pale, slow the tip movement to allow more burning time with each stroke. An early dark tone may mean that you need to move the tool more quickly to achieve a medium tonal value.

6 **The thin background line** is filled with a tightly packed spot that is created by touching the tool tip to the board and then lifting. This touch-and-lift action creates small dark dots on your board (see Square 56 on page 9).

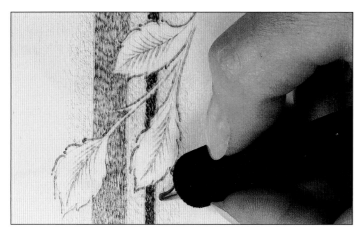

7 **To develop a small amount of contrast color**, or tone, in the background behind the white, unburned areas of the leaves, a curled line or circular stroke is used with a quick, flowing motion. Faster movements with your tool tips burn very pale shades of brown. I found it easier to turn the board upside down for this step.

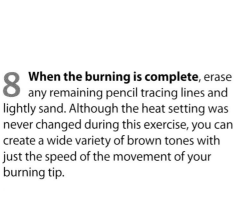

8 **When the burning is complete**, erase any remaining pencil tracing lines and lightly sand. Although the heat setting was never changed during this exercise, you can create a wide variety of brown tones with just the speed of the movement of your burning tip.

Light and Dark Exercise Three: Layers of Strokes

The light and dark areas in the design *Ivy Line,* pattern on page 22, were created by adding layer upon layer of burned strokes to the different areas (see the photos at the right). The number of layers determines the lightness or darkness of each element within the pattern. The simplest stroke for layer work is the tightly spaced crosshatch pattern (see Squares 24–32 on page 9). Here, straight lines are laid down with all of the lines in that layer going in one direction. With each new layer the lines are burned in a new direction. I used a medium heat setting for this exercise.

Tips for completing the entire pattern:

- *Ivy Line* has four different shades of light and dark: There is a very pale set of leaves that uses one layer of lines (1), the medium-colored leaves use two layers (2), the darkest leaves use three layers (3), and the borderline is done in a short-line fill texture (4). This design is not outlined.

- The borderlines are burned using tightly packed spots (see Square 56 on page 9).

Ivy Line. How many layers of texturing you choose to burn determines how dark an area will become. Layering can easily take an area from very pale linen tones to the darkest tones of black.

1 **A simple ivy leaf pattern** is perfect for learning to use layers of burning to create tonal value changes in a project. Add this small design to your practice board.

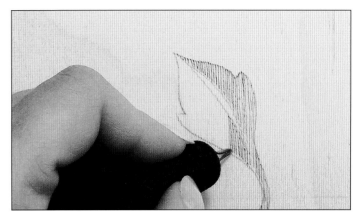

2 **Begin burning** tightly packed parallel lines into both sides of the leaf pattern at a 45-degree angle to the design (see Square 24 on page 9). Space your lines evenly as you work. Notice in the sample that the width of the unburned wood is about the same size as the width of the burned line. Start each line at the top of the pencil tracing line and pull it until it touches the bottom tracing line of that section of leaf.

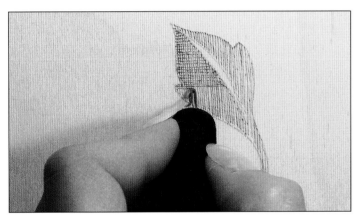

3 **On one side of the leaf,** burn a second layer of tightly packed parallel lines. These lines should run 90 degrees to the lines in your first layer of burning (see Square 25 on page 9). Notice that this second layer makes that side of the leaf darker in tone then the other side.

4 **A third layer of tightly packed parallel lines** has been burned into the dark side of the leaf. This layer is worked at a 45-degree angle to the previous layer (see Square 26 on page 9). You should have two very different colors, or tones, of brown in the two sides of your leaf when you are done with the third layer.

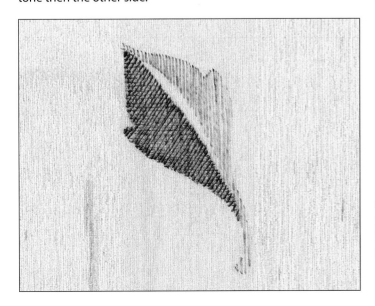

5 **When the work is complete,** erase your pencil lines and lightly sand. Changing the number of layers you burn with crosshatching is a simple and foolproof way to create different tonal values.

Wild Rose Corner
Pattern shown at actual size.

© Lora S. Irish

Ivy Line
Pattern shown at actual size.

© Lora S. Irish

Light and Dark Exercise Four: Texture Pattern

So far in our practice projects we have used straight lines, crosshatching, random curls, and the short-line fill stroke, but any pattern of burning can be used to create the dark and light areas in your woodburning design (see the photos at the right). For *My Room Gingerbread Man*, pattern on page 25, I chose to burn the background areas using three capital letters: A, B, and C (see Square 46 on page 9). Be creative with the texture pattern that you choose for this project. This pattern could easily be done by using 1, 2, 3 or by using a child's name, such as "AMY" or "JEFFREY." The words "My Room" could also be replaced with your child's name. I used a medium setting for this exercise.

The *My Room Gingerbread Man* pattern is too detailed to practice just a part, so we will practice the negative space technique with the letter A. In order to form a negative element, shading must be especially dark on the borders of the object to emphasize and define its edges. I chose random curls for this exercise, but you can choose any fun texture you want!

Tips for completing the entire pattern:

- Although I have burned my sample on a piece of birch plywood, this particular pattern would be delightful done on a gingerbread man cut-out shape or a door hanger sign.

- Using a T-square, ruler, and soft #4B to #6B pencil, mark guidelines across the wood for your letter placement. Because this pattern is fairly tall, I used a spacing of ⅛" (0.5cm).

- When you reach an area on the inner design—the eyes, mouth, icing trim, or words "My Room"—stop burning. Notice with this pattern that the woodburned areas are used to surround the actual important elements of the design.

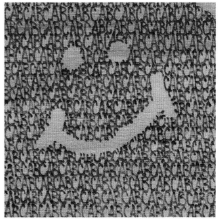

My Room Gingerbread Man. Not only has this design been worked with an unusual texturing pattern, it is also done as a negative pattern, or negative image. The woodburning has been worked to surround the main elements (the lettering and face) of the pattern and therefore make the unburned areas of the gingerbread man stand out.

1 **Add this small pattern** to your practice board.

2 **Working with any of the three techniques** that we are discussing in this section—temperature, burning time, and layers—begin to shade in all of the space surrounding the letter A to a pale or light tone of brown.

3 **As you work, darken the areas** that are nearest the letter A to a medium tone. Notice how the letter begins to stand out from its background even though you have done no woodburning to the letter itself.

4 **Your darkest tonal value** of brown should be where the background directly touches the letter. Don't outline the letter; instead, darken the background.

5 **Erase your guidelines** and pattern lines, and then lightly sand the surface. Dark tonal values can make unburned or unworked areas of your project stand out against their brown backgrounds. Dramatic changes in tonal values create a striking finish for a pattern.

© Lora S. Irish

**My Room
Gingerbread Man**
Pattern shown at actual size.

Light and Dark Exercise Five: Putting It All Together

In *Buffalo Skull Dream Weaver Circle*, pattern on page 28, I have put all of these methods together to create a work that has several points of interest (see the photos at the right). The first thing that you may notice is the dramatic changes in shading. The paleness of the buffalo skull is balanced by the extremely dark surrounding circles of the dream catcher. Second, each area of the woodburning has its own texturing stroke. Because this exercise includes so many different textures and techniques, we will be working with the whole pattern instead of using a portion of the pattern as we did with the previous exercises.

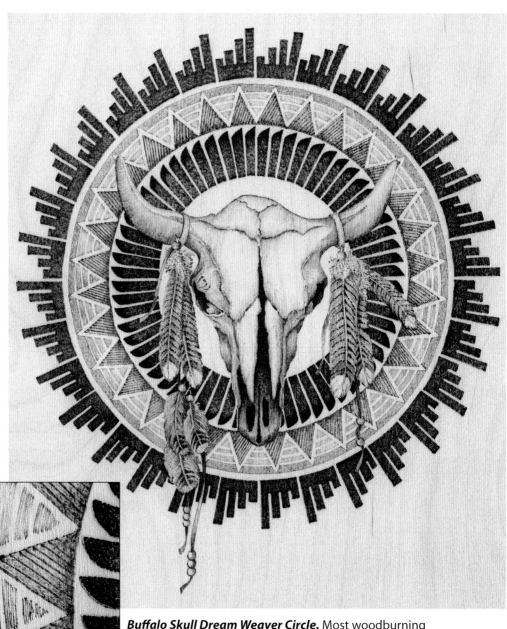

Buffalo Skull Dream Weaver Circle. Most woodburning patterns use temperature, time, texture, and layering to create distinct tonal values. The *Buffalo Skull Dream Weaver Circle* is an excellent pattern to practice and experiment with the four ingredients.

Light and Dark Exercise Five: Putting It All Together *(continued)*

1 The outer ring was created by using tightly packed, straight, diagonal lines; a medium-high temperature; and a slow rate of movement. Several layers of this stroke were burned until the area had a dark, even coloring.

2 The next ring is made of short, straight-line fill strokes (see Square 66 on page 9) on a medium temperature and with a medium time for burning, while the inner sections of the pie-shaped wedges are straight lines. The inner pie wedges were first darkly burned with widely spaced, straight, diagonal lines (see Square 15 on page 9). Then, layers of random curls (see Squares 33–37 on page 9) were applied over the lines. Once a medium-dark tone was achieved, one more layering of random curls was added along the inner edge of the circle to deepen this line.

3 The last ring is made up of feather-shaped curved-line strokes (see Squares 69–70 on page 9). These were burned at a high temperature setting and with a small dash stroke pattern (see Squares 1–5 on page 9) by letting the tool tip rest for a moment to create the dark tone. Along the outer edge of this feather shape, a second layer of dash stroke pattern was added to darken the tips to a black coloring.

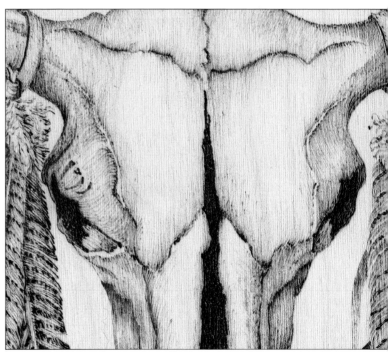

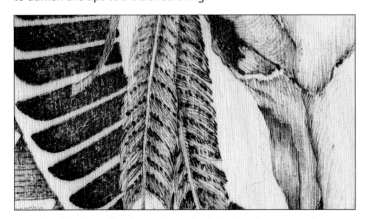

4 The buffalo skull design was burned using a fine-line texturing at low temperatures. This work is very similar to the work in *Our Daily Bread*. Layer upon layer of fine lines were added to darken the shadows of each area, giving the skull a three-dimensional finish. The black areas within the skull are filled with the small-dot pattern at a high temperature until these areas are as black as the inner circle feather shapes.

5 The feathers that hang from the buffalo's horns are done in short curved-line strokes (see Square 70 on page 9). A central line to the feathers was first burned, and then finer lines were added, working from that centerline out toward the edge of the feather.

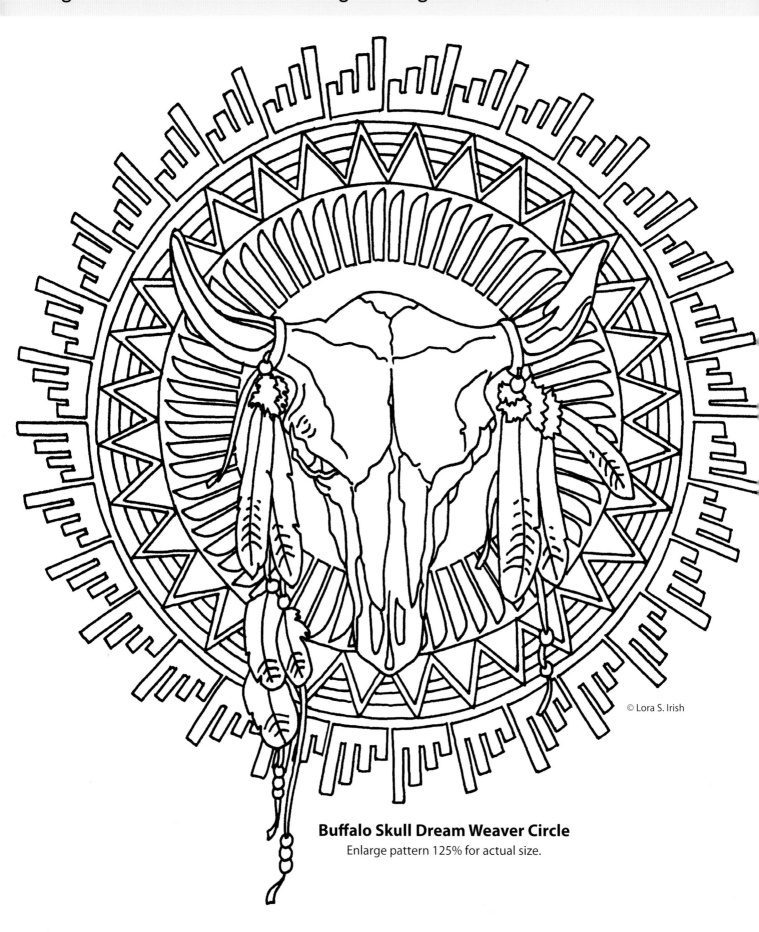

© Lora S. Irish

Buffalo Skull Dream Weaver Circle
Enlarge pattern 125% for actual size.

Texture Exercise: Putting Textures Together

The *Solar Flare Sun Face*, pattern on page 31, is a fun pattern to try if you want to explore the multiple textures that you can use in woodburning (see the photo above). To add to the fun look of *Solar Flare Sun Face*, I chose a very grain-sculptured piece of heartwood birch plywood for the project. Not only is the sun face full of changing patterns and textures, but so is the unburned background of the wood because of its dramatic graining. Try this design using the texture patterns that most interest you from the practice board, as well as experimental texture patterns of your own! Here again, we will be working with the whole pattern instead of using a portion of the pattern as we did with the previous exercises. I used a medium heat setting throughout this exercise.

This design, *Solar Flare Sun Face*, uses eight distinct textures: crosshatching, dash strokes, wavy lines, random curls, seashell circles, herringbone, diagonal lines, and detail outlining. This was all worked on heartwood birch plywood, which adds more texture to the finished design because of the changing grain pattern in the wood.

1 **For my sample, I used tight-spaced crosshatching** (see Squares 24–32 on page 9) to establish the shadows and shading in the face. Adding more layers of crosshatching created the darker facial shadings

2 **Touching the tool tip to the wood** to burn tightly packed, small dots (see Square 56 on page 9) gave the eyes, nostrils, and mouth the black-chocolate coloring.

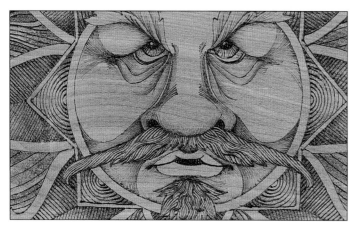

3 **The wavy-line texture** (see Square 42 on page 9) was used to create the sun face's mustache. Over this texturing, a light layering of random curls (see Squares 33–37 on page 9) made the mustache darker where it touched the bottom of the nose.

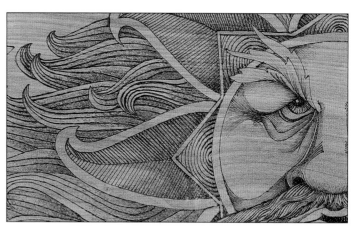

4 **The diamond shapes** that surround the sun face were filled with the seashell circle texture (see Square 43 on page 9).

5 **The sun flare leaves** have a herringbone straight-line burn (see Square 53 on page 9) worked from the centerline out toward the flare's edge. Detail lines were first burned into the curling flares that make up the hair. Over this detailing, random curls (see Squares 33–37 on page 9) were laid to create the shading. New layers of random curls were burned to darken these flares where one flare tucked under another. The stars were filled in with two layers of diagonal lines.

6 **Once all of the texturing and shading were completed**, I added the outline burn to each element.

Solar Flare Sun Face
Enlarge pattern 160% for actual size.

© Lora S. Irish

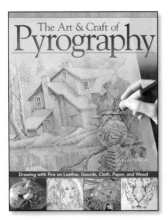
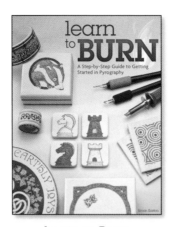

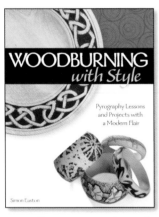

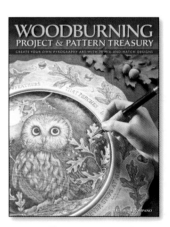